MAD LIBS®
PRESIDENTIAL MAD LIBS

by Douglas Yacka

Mad Libs
An Imprint of Penguin Random House

MAD LIBS
Penguin Young Readers Group
An Imprint of Penguin Random House LLC

Concept created by Roger Price & Leonard Stern

Published by Mad Libs,
an imprint of Penguin Random House LLC,
345 Hudson Street, New York, New York 10014.
Printed in the USA.

ISBN 9781524786182
1 3 5 7 9 10 8 6 4 2

MAD LIBS

INSTRUCTIONS

MAD LIBS® is a game for people who don't like games! It can be played by one, two, three, four, or forty.

• RIDICULOUSLY SIMPLE DIRECTIONS

In this tablet you will find stories containing blank spaces where words are left out. One player, the READER, selects one of these stories. The READER does not tell anyone what the story is about. Instead, he/she asks the other players, the WRITERS, to give him/her words. These words are used to fill in the blank spaces in the story.

• TO PLAY

The READER asks each WRITER in turn to call out a word—an adjective or a noun or whatever the space calls for—and uses them to fill in the blank spaces in the story. The result is a MAD LIBS® game.

When the READER then reads the completed MAD LIBS® game to the other players, they will discover that they have written a story that is fantastic, screamingly funny, shocking, silly, crazy, or just plain dumb—depending upon which words each WRITER called out.

• EXAMPLE (*Before* and *After*)

"_____!" he said _____
    EXCLAMATION   ADVERB

as he jumped into his convertible _____ and
                              NOUN

drove off with his _____ wife.
              ADJECTIVE

"__OUCH__!" he said __STUPIDLY__
    EXCLAMATION   ADVERB

as he jumped into his convertible __CAT__ and
                              NOUN

drove off with his __BRAVE__ wife.
              ADJECTIVE

MAD LIBS

QUICK REVIEW

In case you have forgotten what adjectives, adverbs, nouns, and verbs are, here is a quick review:

An ADJECTIVE describes something or somebody. *Lumpy, soft, ugly, messy,* and *short* are adjectives.

An ADVERB tells how something is done. It modifies a verb and usually ends in "ly." *Modestly, stupidly, greedily,* and *carefully* are adverbs.

A NOUN is the name of a person, place, or thing. *Sidewalk, umbrella, bridle, bathtub,* and *nose* are nouns.

A VERB is an action word. *Run, pitch, jump,* and *swim* are verbs. Put the verbs in past tense if the directions say PAST TENSE. *Ran, pitched, jumped,* and *swam* are verbs in the past tense.

When we ask for A PLACE, we mean any sort of place: a country or city (*Spain, Cleveland*) or a room (*bathroom, kitchen*).

An EXCLAMATION or SILLY WORD is any sort of funny sound, gasp, grunt, or outcry, like *Wow!, Ouch!, Whomp!, Ick!,* and *Gadzooks!*

When we ask for specific words, like a NUMBER, a COLOR, an ANIMAL, or a PART OF THE BODY, we mean a word that is one of those things, like *seven, blue, horse,* or *head.*

When we ask for a PLURAL, it means more than one. For example, *cat* pluralized is *cats.*

MAD LIBS® is fun to play with friends, but you can also play it by yourself! To begin with, DO NOT look at the story on the page below. Fill in the blanks on this page with the words called for. Then, using the words you have selected, fill in the blank spaces in the story.

Now you've created your own hilarious MAD LIBS® game!

SO, YOU WANT TO BE PRESIDENT?

NOUN _____

ADJECTIVE _____

A PLACE _____

OCCUPATION _____

PART OF THE BODY (PLURAL) _____

ADJECTIVE _____

PLURAL NOUN _____

NOUN _____

PART OF THE BODY _____

ADJECTIVE _____

VERB (PAST TENSE) _____

ADVERB _____

PART OF THE BODY (PLURAL) _____

VERB ENDING IN "ING" _____

NOUN _____

MAD LIBS
SO, YOU WANT TO BE PRESIDENT?

Do you dream of becoming the next _____ of the United

NOUN

States? You'll probably want to start with a/an _____ position,

ADJECTIVE

like a councilperson or mayor of (the) _____ . Then you

A PLACE

could become a state representative or a/an _____ in order to

OCCUPATION

cut your legislative _____ ! Just make sure you don't

PART OF THE BODY (PLURAL)

support any _____ bills or controversial _____ .

ADJECTIVE · PLURAL NOUN

When in doubt, always side with the everyday _____ . Be sure

NOUN

to keep your _____ clean and stay free of _____

PART OF THE BODY · ADJECTIVE

scandals, which will be sure to surface during your campaign.

Everything you've ever said or _____ will come to

VERB (PAST TENSE)

light. Finally, learn to smile and wave _____ . You'll be shaking

ADVERB

a lot of _____ and _____ a

PART OF THE BODY (PLURAL) · VERB ENDING IN "ING"

lot of babies on the campaign trail! Or you could always start as a

reality TV _____ !

NOUN

MAD LIBS® is fun to play with friends, but you can also play it by yourself! To begin with, DO NOT look at the story on the page below. Fill in the blanks on this page with the words called for. Then, using the words you have selected, fill in the blank spaces in the story.

Now you've created your own hilarious MAD LIBS® game!

PRESIDENTIAL FIRSTS

NOUN _____

VERB _____

ARTICLE OF CLOTHING (PLURAL) _____

PART OF THE BODY (PLURAL) _____

NOUN _____

VERB (PAST TENSE) _____

PLURAL NOUN _____

ADJECTIVE _____

PART OF THE BODY (PLURAL) _____

NOUN _____

PLURAL NOUN _____

ADJECTIVE _____

VERB _____

NOUN _____

MAD LIBS

PRESIDENTIAL FIRSTS

John Adams was the first _____ to live in the White House.

NOUN

James Madison was the first to _____ in long pants. Before that,

VERB

the gentlemen of the time wore _____ covering

ARTICLE OF CLOTHING (PLURAL)

their _____. **James Monroe** was the first to ride on

PART OF THE BODY (PLURAL)

a/an _____-ship. It is said that he felt queasy and

NOUN

_____ all over the deck. **Rutherford B. Hayes** was the

VERB (PAST TENSE)

first to ban alcoholic _____ from the White House. The first

PLURAL NOUN

_____-handed president was **James A. Garfield**, although he

ADJECTIVE

learned how to write with both _____. **Benjamin**

PART OF THE BODY (PLURAL)

Harrison was the first to have electricity in his _____, but he

NOUN

was afraid to turn the _____ on and off. **William Howard**

PLURAL NOUN

Taft was the first to throw the ceremonial _____ pitch at a

ADJECTIVE

baseball game. **Franklin D. Roosevelt** was the first president to

_____ on TV. These days, you can't turn on the _____

VERB _____ NOUN

without seeing our president!

MAD LIBS® is fun to play with friends, but you can also play it by yourself! To begin with, DO NOT look at the story on the page below. Fill in the blanks on this page with the words called for. Then, using the words you have selected, fill in the blank spaces in the story.

Now you've created your own hilarious MAD LIBS® game!

AIR FORCE ONE

A PLACE _____

PLURAL NOUN _____

NUMBER _____

VERB ENDING IN "ING" _____

PLURAL NOUN _____

ADJECTIVE _____

VERB ENDING IN "ING" _____

ADJECTIVE _____

ADJECTIVE _____

ADJECTIVE _____

VERB _____

NOUN _____

ADJECTIVE _____

ADJECTIVE _____

OCCUPATION (PLURAL) _____

MAD LIBS

AIR FORCE ONE

There is no plane in (the) _____ more famous than Air Force
                                 A PLACE

One. Many _____ do not realize this, but there are actually
                PLURAL NOUN

_____ planes with this designation. "Air Force One" refers to
    NUMBER

whichever plane the president is _____ on at the
                                    VERB ENDING IN "ING"

moment. The plane is quite large, with four thousand square

_____ , including an office, a bedroom, two _____
    PLURAL NOUN   ADJECTIVE

kitchens, and a/an _____ room. Stylish and
                      VERB ENDING IN "ING"

_____ décor was added when Jackie Kennedy was First Lady.
    ADJECTIVE

Also on board is a mobile Situation Room in case of a/an _____
                                                              ADJECTIVE

emergency, and even a flying hospital. Security is a/an _____
                                                           ADJECTIVE

concern, so the plane can _____ enemy signals and deflect
                               VERB

weapons. It is rumored that the plane can act as a/an _____
                                                          NOUN

bunker in case of a/an _____ attack. In addition to the
                          ADJECTIVE

president's staff, members of the _____ press are often on board.
                                      ADJECTIVE

Even in the air, the president can't escape from _____ !
                                                  OCCUPATION (PLURAL)

MAD LIBS® is fun to play with friends, but you can also play it by yourself! To begin with, DO NOT look at the story on the page below. Fill in the blanks on this page with the words called for. Then, using the words you have selected, fill in the blank spaces in the story.

Now you've created your own hilarious MAD LIBS® game!

TO TRUMP OR NOT TO TRUMP

VERB _____

ADJECTIVE _____

ARTICLE OF CLOTHING (PLURAL) _____

VERB ENDING IN "ING" _____

NOUN _____

ADJECTIVE _____

TYPE OF BUILDING (PLURAL) _____

PLURAL NOUN _____

VERB ENDING IN "ING" _____

OCCUPATION (PLURAL) _____

PLURAL NOUN _____

CELEBRITY _____

VERB _____

PLURAL NOUN _____

MAD LIBS
TO TRUMP OR NOT TO TRUMP

Dan: Did you really _____ for Trump? I had no idea.
VERB

Joe: Sure. I don't know why everyone acts so _____ when I
ADJECTIVE

say that. I even have one of those red _____
ARTICLE OF CLOTHING (PLURAL)

with his slogan on it.

Dan: Doesn't it bother you that he is always _____
VERB ENDING IN "ING"

himself and acts like he's the best _____ in the world?
NOUN

Joe: I think it shows how _____ he is. Remember how successful he
ADJECTIVE

was in building _____ and managing _____?
TYPE OF BUILDING (PLURAL)   PLURAL NOUN

Dan: But aren't you worried about him _____ with
VERB ENDING IN "ING"

foreign countries?

Joe: I think foreign _____ will respect his views on
OCCUPATION (PLURAL)

_____ . And he's much more persuasive than _____!
PLURAL NOUN   CELEBRITY

Dan: Well, we should really _____ back to work, since we are
VERB

both _____ in his cabinet.
PLURAL NOUN

MAD LIBS® is fun to play with friends, but you can also play it by yourself! To begin with, DO NOT look at the story on the page below. Fill in the blanks on this page with the words called for. Then, using the words you have selected, fill in the blank spaces in the story.

Now you've created your own hilarious MAD LIBS® game!

BAD, BAD BOYS

ADJECTIVE _____

NOUN _____

NOUN _____

TYPE OF EVENT _____

ADJECTIVE _____

PLURAL NOUN _____

TYPE OF LIQUID _____

PLURAL NOUN _____

TYPE OF LIQUID _____

NOUN _____

PLURAL NOUN _____

VERB ENDING IN "ING" _____

CELEBRITY (FEMALE) _____

VERB (PAST TENSE) _____

TYPE OF BUILDING _____

VERB _____

MAD LIBS®

BAD, BAD BOYS

We tend to think of our presidents as upstanding, distinguished, and

_____ figures leading the country. But some have gotten into
   ADJECTIVE

a/an _____ -load of trouble.
        NOUN

Andrew Jackson married a woman who was already married to another

_____ . Also, Jackson's inauguration _____ got so
       NOUN   TYPE OF EVENT

_____ that crowds broke dishes and _____ in the
   ADJECTIVE   PLURAL NOUN

White House. **Ulysses S. Grant's** administration stole taxes from the

sale of _____ , while **Warren G. Harding's** _____
        TYPE OF LIQUID   PLURAL NOUN

sold the rights to drill for _____ . **Andrew Johnson** was
                              TYPE OF LIQUID

the first _____ to be impeached for illegally firing his secretary of
            NOUN

_____ . **Bill Clinton** was also impeached for _____
PLURAL NOUN   VERB ENDING IN "ING"

under oath about his affair with _____ . But the most
                                  CELEBRITY (FEMALE)

famous scandal is Watergate, where **Richard Nixon** _____
                                                      VERB (PAST TENSE)

to cover up a break-in at the Democratic _____ . He wound
                                          TYPE OF BUILDING

up having to _____ in disgrace!
                VERB

MAD LIBS® is fun to play with friends, but you can also play it by yourself! To begin with, DO NOT look at the story on the page below. Fill in the blanks on this page with the words called for. Then, using the words you have selected, fill in the blank spaces in the story.

Now you've created your own hilarious MAD LIBS® game!

HAIL TO THE CHIEF

ADJECTIVE _____

VERB _____

NOUN _____

CELEBRITY (MALE) _____

VERB ENDING IN "ING" _____

ADJECTIVE _____

ADJECTIVE _____

NOUN _____

PERSON IN ROOM _____

NOUN _____

ADJECTIVE _____

PLURAL NOUN _____

A PLACE _____

OCCUPATION _____

NOUN _____

VERB _____

PLURAL NOUN _____

ADJECTIVE _____

MAD LIBS®

HAIL TO THE CHIEF

Imagine having your own _____ anthem that plays almost
                            ADJECTIVE

everywhere you _____! As president, you get to hear it at
                     VERB

every _____ you attend. Every president since _____
           NOUN   CELEBRITY (MALE)

has used the song when _____ at special occasions,
                          VERB ENDING IN "ING"

with the exception of Chester A. Arthur, who thought it was

_____, and had a different song called " _____
   ADJECTIVE   ADJECTIVE

_____ " written just for him. "Hail to the Chief" was adapted
   NOUN

from a poem by _____ called "The _____ of the
                 PERSON IN ROOM   NOUN

Lake." Although the _____ tune is well known, many
                       ADJECTIVE

_____ do not know the lyrics:
   PLURAL NOUN

Hail to the Chief we have chosen for (the) _____,
                                              A PLACE

Hail to the _____! We salute him, _____ and all.
               OCCUPATION   NOUN

_____ to the Chief, as we pledge _____,
      VERB   PLURAL NOUN

In proud fulfillment of a great, _____ call!
                                     ADJECTIVE

MAD LIBS® is fun to play with friends, but you can also play it by yourself! To begin with, DO NOT look at the story on the page below. Fill in the blanks on this page with the words called for. Then, using the words you have selected, fill in the blank spaces in the story.

Now you've created your own hilarious MAD LIBS® game!

PRESIDENTIAL PETS

NOUN _____

NOUN _____

ADJECTIVE _____

ANIMAL _____

VERB ENDING IN "ING" _____

COLOR _____

ADJECTIVE _____

VERB _____

ADJECTIVE _____

VERB (PAST TENSE) _____

ADVERB _____

ADJECTIVE _____

NOUN _____

ADJECTIVE _____

ANIMAL _____

MAD LIBS®

PRESIDENTIAL PETS

Even the most powerful _____ in the world likes to snuggle
                              NOUN

up with a cuddly _____ every now and then. The White
                   NOUN

House has had many furry, feathered, and _____ pets through
                                          ADJECTIVE

the years. Of course, the most popular is man's best friend, the

_____ . Every president since Theodore Roosevelt has had a
   ANIMAL

dog _____ through the halls of the _____
    VERB ENDING IN "ING"   COLOR

House. Cats are also among the most _____ of choices. You
                                      ADJECTIVE

might _____ , though, if you knew some of the more
        VERB

_____ critters on the list. Both Herbert Hoover and John
  ADJECTIVE

Quincy Adams _____ alligators in the White House
              VERB (PAST TENSE)

(Adams enjoyed _____ scaring visitors with his gator).
                 ADVERB

Theodore Roosevelt was given a/an _____ bear, and Martin
                                   ADJECTIVE

Van Buren was given two tigers as a gift in place of a/an _____ .
                                                            NOUN

However, the most _____ pet owner was probably Calvin
                    ADJECTIVE

Coolidge, who had a wallaby, a/an _____ , and a hippopotamus!
                                     ANIMAL

MAD LIBS® is fun to play with friends, but you can also play it by yourself! To begin with, DO NOT look at the story on the page below. Fill in the blanks on this page with the words called for. Then, using the words you have selected, fill in the blank spaces in the story.

Now you've created your own hilarious MAD LIBS® game!

THE VETO

PLURAL NOUN _____

VERB _____

PLURAL NOUN _____

NOUN _____

VERB _____

A PLACE _____

VERB _____

NUMBER _____

NOUN _____

ADJECTIVE _____

PART OF THE BODY (PLURAL) _____

PLURAL NOUN _____

ADJECTIVE _____

ADJECTIVE _____

MAD LIBS

THE VETO

One of the special _____ that a president has is the ability to
<u>PLURAL NOUN</u>

_____ a bill before it becomes a law. After a bill is approved by
<u>VERB</u>

the Senate and the House of _____ , it makes its way to the
<u>PLURAL NOUN</u>

president's _____ to be signed. If the president does not want
<u>NOUN</u>

to _____ the bill, he or she can use the veto and send it back
<u>VERB</u>

to (the) _____ to be reconsidered. Congress can then
<u>A PLACE</u>

_____ the president if _____ of them vote to
<u>VERB</u>   <u>NUMBER</u>

override, in which case the _____ becomes law. This will
<u>NOUN</u>

probably make the president _____ . In certain cases, it's been
<u>ADJECTIVE</u>

said that presidents have become so upset that smoke came out of their

_____ ! The reason for the veto is to keep the
<u>PART OF THE BODY (PLURAL)</u>

_____ of the government from having too much
<u>PLURAL NOUN</u>

_____ power. But by using it, one side will always end up the
<u>ADJECTIVE</u>

_____ loser!
<u>ADJECTIVE</u>

MAD LIBS® is fun to play with friends, but you can also play it by yourself! To begin with, DO NOT look at the story on the page below. Fill in the blanks on this page with the words called for. Then, using the words you have selected, fill in the blank spaces in the story.

Now you've created your own hilarious MAD LIBS® game!

HOME SWEET HOME

ADJECTIVE _____

NUMBER _____

NOUN _____

CELEBRITY (MALE) _____

NUMBER _____

NOUN _____

VERB ENDING IN "ING" _____

PLURAL NOUN _____

PART OF THE BODY _____

TYPE OF FOOD _____

TYPE OF FOOD _____

ADJECTIVE _____

ADJECTIVE _____

PLURAL NOUN _____

PLURAL NOUN _____

ADJECTIVE _____

PLURAL NOUN _____

MAD LIBS®

HOME SWEET HOME

Thank you for joining us this morning as we take you on a/an

_____ tour of the White House. Over _____ people
  ADJECTIVE   NUMBER

visit this _____ every year. The first president to live here was
           NOUN

_____. The house itself has 132 rooms, including
 CELEBRITY (MALE)

_____ bathrooms, a movie theater, a bowling _____,
 NUMBER   NOUN

and a/an _____ pool. There is a staff of about ninety
       VERB ENDING IN "ING"

_____ ready to wait on the president hand and _____,
 PLURAL NOUN   PART OF THE BODY

including five chefs to cook everything from _____ to
                                       TYPE OF FOOD

_____. The most well-known area of the building is the
 TYPE OF FOOD

_____ Wing, where we find the president's famous
   ADJECTIVE

_____ Office. Important _____ are discussed here,
  ADJECTIVE   PLURAL NOUN

where many historic _____ have been signed through the
             PLURAL NOUN

years. Standing here, you really feel a/an _____ sense of
                                 ADJECTIVE

history. Plus, you can brag about your house to the _____
                                         PLURAL NOUN

next door!

MAD LIBS® is fun to play with friends, but you can also play it by yourself! To begin with, DO NOT look at the story on the page below. Fill in the blanks on this page with the words called for. Then, using the words you have selected, fill in the blank spaces in the story.

Now you've created your own hilarious MAD LIBS® game!

HONEST ABE

PLURAL NOUN _____

ADVERB _____

VERB ENDING IN "ING" _____

PERSON IN ROOM _____

NUMBER _____

PART OF THE BODY (PLURAL) _____

PLURAL NOUN _____

ADJECTIVE _____

OCCUPATION _____

ANIMAL (PLURAL) _____

VERB _____

ADJECTIVE _____

VERB ENDING IN "ING" _____

OCCUPATION (PLURAL) _____

NOUN _____

ADJECTIVE _____

MAD LIBS

HONEST ABE

Few _____ are as revered as Abraham Lincoln, known
        PLURAL NOUN

_____ for his honesty. "Honest Abe" earned his nickname
      ADVERB

when he was a young man _____ at a general store.
                              VERB ENDING IN "ING"

When he discovered that he had shorted _____ by
                                          PERSON IN ROOM

_____ pennies, he closed the shop and ran as fast as his
      NUMBER

_____ could carry him to return the money! Local
PART OF THE BODY (PLURAL)

_____ started asking Abe to settle _____ disputes
    PLURAL NOUN   ADJECTIVE

and contests. Lincoln was interested in the law and became a respected

_____ . At the time, most lawyers and politicians were considered
OCCUPATION

lying _____ . When Lincoln would _____ in the
       ANIMAL (PLURAL)   VERB

courthouse, even those who lost to him still respected his _____
                                                              ADJECTIVE

integrity. As president, Lincoln was known for _____
                                                  VERB ENDING IN "ING"

the truth to his generals and _____ . His honesty became
                               OCCUPATION (PLURAL)

the _____ of American virtue. And that's the _____
        NOUN   ADJECTIVE

truth!

From PRESIDENTIAL MAD LIBS® • Copyright © 2017 by Penguin Random House LLC.

MAD LIBS® is fun to play with friends, but you can also play it by yourself! To begin with, DO NOT look at the story on the page below. Fill in the blanks on this page with the words called for. Then, using the words you have selected, fill in the blank spaces in the story.

Now you've created your own hilarious MAD LIBS® game!

PRESIDENTIAL PRESS CONFERENCE

NOUN _____

NOUN _____

VERB ENDING IN "ING" _____

NOUN _____

PART OF THE BODY _____

NOUN _____

VERB _____

OCCUPATION (PLURAL) _____

PLURAL NOUN _____

FOREIGN COUNTRY _____

ADJECTIVE _____

CELEBRITY _____

ADJECTIVE _____

EXCLAMATION _____

PLURAL NOUN _____

MAD LIBS
PRESIDENTIAL PRESS
CONFERENCE

P: I'd now like to open up the _____ for questions.
<u>NOUN</u>

Q: Can we get your reaction to yesterday's _____ ?
<u>NOUN</u>

P: We are _____ into the matter and will release an
<u>VERB ENDING IN "ING"</u>

official _____ within the next few days.
<u>NOUN</u>

Q: Does that mean you've changed your _____ ?
<u>PART OF THE BODY</u>

P: We stand by our current _____ , but reserve the right to
<u>NOUN</u>

_____ if necessary.
<u>VERB</u>

Q: How do you respond to allegations that _____ in
<u>OCCUPATION (PLURAL)</u>

your cabinet traded _____ with _____ ?
<u>PLURAL NOUN</u>   <u>FOREIGN COUNTRY</u>

P: I have no comment on this _____ accusation.
<u>ADJECTIVE</u>

Q: Do you disagree with the statement made by _____ , who
<u>CELEBRITY</u>

called your remarks _____ ?
<u>ADJECTIVE</u>

P: _____ ! I do not need the opinions of Hollywood
<u>EXCLAMATION</u>

_____ to run the country. No more questions!
<u>PLURAL NOUN</u>

MAD LIBS® is fun to play with friends, but you can also play it by yourself! To begin with, DO NOT look at the story on the page below. Fill in the blanks on this page with the words called for. Then, using the words you have selected, fill in the blank spaces in the story.

Now you've created your own hilarious MAD LIBS® game!

A LETTER FROM GEORGE

PLURAL NOUN _____

OCCUPATION _____

A PLACE _____

NUMBER _____

ADJECTIVE _____

VERB ENDING IN "ING" _____

PLURAL NOUN _____

A PLACE _____

ADJECTIVE _____

PLURAL NOUN _____

VERB ENDING IN "ING" _____

PLURAL NOUN _____

ADJECTIVE _____

NOUN _____

PART OF THE BODY _____

VERB _____

ADJECTIVE _____

PART OF THE BODY _____

MAD LIBS

A LETTER FROM GEORGE

Hello, my fellow _____ in 2017, it's me, George Washington,
$\quad$ PLURAL NOUN

the first _____ . I am writing from (the) _____ , where
$\quad$ OCCUPATION $\qquad$ A PLACE

I have been secretly living for the past _____ years. I am
$\qquad$ NUMBER

concerned by the _____ state of affairs in America these days.
$\qquad$ ADJECTIVE

It seems that your politicians are more concerned with

_____ one another than with listening to the
VERB ENDING IN "ING"

_____ of the people. When we declared our independence
PLURAL NOUN

from (the) _____ , we set forth on a/an _____ path
$\quad$ A PLACE $\qquad$ ADJECTIVE

guided by the voices of the everyday _____ . If we're going to
$\qquad$ PLURAL NOUN

keep _____ , then we need to learn how to respect all
VERB ENDING IN "ING"

_____ . Don't get me wrong; we had _____ problems
PLURAL NOUN $\qquad$ ADJECTIVE

in my day, too. Benjamin Franklin once called me a/an _____
$\qquad$ NOUN

and kicked me in the _____ . But at the end of the day, we
PART OF THE BODY

were able to _____ in harmony. Let us find that _____
$\quad$ VERB $\qquad$ ADJECTIVE

spirit once again, or else I'm taking my _____ off the quarter!
PART OF THE BODY

MAD LIBS® is fun to play with friends, but you can also play it by yourself! To begin with, DO NOT look at the story on the page below. Fill in the blanks on this page with the words called for. Then, using the words you have selected, fill in the blank spaces in the story.

Now you've created your own hilarious MAD LIBS® game!

IN THE IMMORTAL WORDS OF ...

NOUN _____

ADJECTIVE _____

VERB _____

VERB _____

NOUN _____

NOUN _____

VERB _____

PART OF THE BODY _____

ADVERB _____

NOUN _____

CELEBRITY (MALE) _____

NOUN _____

PART OF THE BODY _____

PART OF THE BODY _____

NOUN _____

MAD LIBS®
IN THE IMMORTAL
WORDS OF . . .

- "The only thing we have to fear is _____ itself."
  <u>NOUN</u>
  —Franklin D. Roosevelt

- "A president's hardest task is not to do what is _____,
  <u>ADJECTIVE</u>
  but to _____ what is right." —Lyndon B. Johnson
  <u>VERB</u>

- "Ask not what your country can _____ for you—ask
  <u>VERB</u>
  what you can do for your _____." —John F. Kennedy
  <u>NOUN</u>

- "A/An _____ divided against itself cannot
  <u>NOUN</u>
  _____." —Abraham Lincoln
  <u>VERB</u>

- "Read my _____: no new taxes." —George H. W. Bush
  <u>PART OF THE BODY</u>

- "Speak _____ and carry a big _____."
  <u>ADVERB</u>   <u>NOUN</u>
  —Theodore Roosevelt

- "Mr. _____, tear down this _____!"
  <u>CELEBRITY (MALE)</u>   <u>NOUN</u>
  —Ronald Reagan

- "We will extend a/an _____ if you are willing to
  <u>PART OF THE BODY</u>
  unclench your _____." —Barack Obama
  <u>PART OF THE BODY</u>

- "I'm not a/an _____!" —Richard Nixon
  <u>NOUN</u>

MAD LIBS® is fun to play with friends, but you can also play it by yourself! To begin with, DO NOT look at the story on the page below. Fill in the blanks on this page with the words called for. Then, using the words you have selected, fill in the blank spaces in the story.

Now you've created your own hilarious MAD LIBS® game!

EXCERPT FROM TRUMP'S DIARY

ADJECTIVE _____

VERB ENDING IN "ING" _____

ADJECTIVE _____

OCCUPATION _____

PLURAL NOUN _____

NOUN _____

ADVERB _____

ADJECTIVE _____

VERB _____

ADJECTIVE _____

VERB _____

VERB _____

PART OF THE BODY _____

A PLACE _____

VERB ENDING IN "ING" _____

PLURAL NOUN _____

NOUN _____

Dear Diary,

Today was yet another _____ day at the White House. Who
                          ADJECTIVE

knew _____ the country would be so _____?
     VERB ENDING IN "ING"   ADJECTIVE

When I was a/an _____, I had tremendous success in building
                 OCCUPATION

_____. I also liked being a reality TV _____, but
PLURAL NOUN   NOUN

this is _____ different. There are all of these _____
        ADVERB   ADJECTIVE

rules, and everyone seems to _____ them except me. To make
                             VERB

matters worse, I am surrounded by a million _____ people
                                            ADJECTIVE

telling me to _____ one moment and then _____
              VERB   VERB

the next. I feel like my _____ is spinning. And finally, I wish
                         PART OF THE BODY

the press would go to (the) _____ and leave me alone. They
                            A PLACE

are constantly _____ my every move and asking me
               VERB ENDING IN "ING"

about my _____. What kind of _____ have I gotten
          PLURAL NOUN   NOUN

myself into?!

Proudly yours,

Donald

MAD LIBS® is fun to play with friends, but you can also play it by yourself! To begin with, DO NOT look at the story on the page below. Fill in the blanks on this page with the words called for. Then, using the words you have selected, fill in the blank spaces in the story.

Now you've created your own hilarious MAD LIBS® game!

SECOND TO NONE

ADJECTIVE _____

ADJECTIVE _____

PART OF THE BODY _____

NOUN _____

OCCUPATION _____

VERB ENDING IN "ING" _____

PLURAL NOUN _____

VERB _____

VERB ENDING IN "ING" _____

NOUN _____

ADJECTIVE _____

PLURAL NOUN _____

PLURAL NOUN _____

VERB ENDING IN "ING" _____

TYPE OF FOOD _____

ADJECTIVE _____

MAD LIBS

SECOND TO NONE

America's First Ladies have been as _____ as the presidents
                                   ADJECTIVE

themselves. Martha Washington was so _____ that they put
                                      ADJECTIVE

her _____ on the one-dollar bill briefly. Abigail Adams, no
    PART OF THE BODY

less of a/an _____ , was referred to as Mrs. _____ .
             NOUN   OCCUPATION

Some of these ladies liked _____ parties. John Tyler's
                           VERB ENDING IN "ING"

wife, Julia, was fond of lavish _____ . She was even known to
                                PLURAL NOUN

_____ a polka dance! Florence Harding was known for
VERB

_____ strong cocktails, and Lucy Hayes started the
VERB ENDING IN "ING"

annual Easter _____ hunt on the White House lawn. Many
              NOUN

championed _____ causes. Abigail Fillmore loved to read
           ADJECTIVE

_____ and created the White House library. Lucretia Garfield
PLURAL NOUN

campaigned for women to be paid the same as _____ . Laura
                                             PLURAL NOUN

Bush believed in _____ for education, and Michelle
                 VERB ENDING IN "ING"

Obama taught kids to eat their _____ instead of cookies. As
                               TYPE OF FOOD

the saying goes, behind every _____ man is a great woman!
                              ADJECTIVE

MAD LIBS® is fun to play with friends, but you can also play it by yourself! To begin with, DO NOT look at the story on the page below. Fill in the blanks on this page with the words called for. Then, using the words you have selected, fill in the blank spaces in the story.

Now you've created your own hilarious MAD LIBS® game!

ROOSEVELT VS. ROOSEVELT

PLURAL NOUN _____

ADJECTIVE _____

NUMBER _____

PLURAL NOUN _____

VERB ENDING IN "ING" _____

ADJECTIVE _____

OCCUPATION (PLURAL) _____

ADVERB _____

ANIMAL _____

NUMBER _____

ADJECTIVE _____

ADJECTIVE _____

ADJECTIVE _____

PART OF THE BODY _____

PERSON IN ROOM _____

MAD LIBS®

ROOSEVELT VS. ROOSEVELT

Theodore "Teddy" Roosevelt: Many _____ confuse us, but
                                      PLURAL NOUN

Franklin and I couldn't be more _____ .
                                    ADJECTIVE

Franklin D. Roosevelt: True. For starters, our presidencies were

_____ years apart.
   NUMBER

Teddy: I liked to be outside, enjoying the _____ of nature,
                                                  PLURAL NOUN

while you were always _____ indoors.
                        VERB ENDING IN "ING"

FDR: I brought America out of the _____ Depression. Let's
                                         ADJECTIVE

not forget how many _____ I put back to work.
                       OCCUPATION (PLURAL)

Teddy: Well, I fought _____ against big businesses, so you
                              ADVERB

can get off your high _____ !
                          ANIMAL

FDR: I also had to deal with World War _____ . Do you
                                              NUMBER

think that was a/an _____ task?
                       ADJECTIVE

Teddy: I wouldn't know. I kept the world a much more _____
                                                            ADJECTIVE

place as president.

FDR: Don't be _____ . They put my _____ on the dime.
                    ADJECTIVE   PART OF THE BODY

Teddy: Dimes are small. My giant face is on the side of Mt.

_____ . Looks like I win!
PERSON IN ROOM

MAD LIBS® is fun to play with friends, but you can also play it by yourself! To begin with, DO NOT look at the story on the page below. Fill in the blanks on this page with the words called for. Then, using the words you have selected, fill in the blank spaces in the story.

Now you've created your own hilarious MAD LIBS® game!

TWEETS FROM THE TOP

A PLACE _____

TYPE OF EVENT _____

NOUN _____

ADJECTIVE _____

EXCLAMATION _____

NOUN _____

OCCUPATION (PLURAL) _____

PLURAL NOUN _____

CELEBRITY (MALE) _____

ADJECTIVE _____

PART OF THE BODY _____

PLURAL NOUN _____

ADJECTIVE _____

MAD LIBS®

TWEETS FROM THE TOP

Donald J. Trump @surrealDonaldTrump • 6m

Holding a big rally in (the) _____ this afternoon. Biggest

A PLACE

crowd since the presidential _____!

TYPE OF EVENT

Donald J. Trump @surrealDonaldTrump • 7m

Reports of a/an _____ scandal totally untrue. Everything

NOUN

here at the White House is totally _____ . #_____!

ADJECTIVE   EXCLAMATION

Donald J. Trump @surrealDonaldTrump • 5h

_____ growth is the biggest it's been in a decade,

NOUN

_____ say. Bringing _____ back to America!

OCCUPATION (PLURAL)   PLURAL NOUN

Donald J. Trump @surrealDonaldTrump • 7h

Comments by @ _____ totally _____! He is

CELEBRITY (MALE)   ADJECTIVE

losing his _____ . #canttouchthis

PART OF THE BODY

Donald J. Trump @surrealDonaldTrump • 9h

Don't believe the _____ . We are making America

PLURAL NOUN

_____ again!

ADJECTIVE

MAD LIBS® is fun to play with friends, but you can also play it by yourself! To begin with, DO NOT look at the story on the page below. Fill in the blanks on this page with the words called for. Then, using the words you have selected, fill in the blank spaces in the story.

Now you've created your own hilarious MAD LIBS® game!

DID YOU KNOW...?

NUMBER _____

NOUN _____

NOUN _____

ADJECTIVE _____

VERB ENDING IN "ING" _____

NOUN _____

NOUN _____

NOUN _____

TYPE OF LIQUID _____

ADJECTIVE _____

MAD LIBS

DID YOU KNOW . . . ?

- James Madison was our shortest president, at only five feet
  _____ inches tall.
  NUMBER

- Barack Obama was a collector of _____ books, such as
  NOUN
  Conan the _____ and *Spider-Man*.
  NOUN

- William Howard Taft was so _____ that he got stuck
  ADJECTIVE
  in the White House bathtub.

- The record for _____ to other countries belongs
  VERB ENDING IN "ING"
  to Bill Clinton.

- Chester A. Arthur was known as " _____ Arthur"
  NOUN
  because of his sense of fashion.

- Four presidents have received the Nobel _____ Prize.
  NOUN

- William Henry Harrison died exactly one month after taking
  the _____ of office.
  NOUN

- George Washington owned a/an _____ distillery.
  TYPE OF LIQUID
  That explains why his portraits look so _____!
  ADJECTIVE

MAD LIBS® is fun to play with friends, but you can also play it by yourself! To begin with, DO NOT look at the story on the page below. Fill in the blanks on this page with the words called for. Then, using the words you have selected, fill in the blank spaces in the story.

Now you've created your own hilarious MAD LIBS® game!

THOSE ARE THE PERKS

NOUN _____

ADJECTIVE _____

VEHICLE _____

NOUN _____

NUMBER _____

ADJECTIVE _____

TYPE OF FOOD _____

TYPE OF FOOD (PLURAL) _____

OCCUPATION _____

ADJECTIVE _____

PART OF THE BODY _____

PERSON IN ROOM _____

VERB _____

PLURAL NOUN _____

PLURAL NOUN _____

MAD LIBS®

THOSE ARE THE PERKS

Aside from being the most powerful _____ in the world, you
                                        NOUN

also get a/an _____ number of perks as president. Your
                ADJECTIVE

_____, nicknamed "The _____," is the safest there
   VEHICLE   NOUN

is. You are also surrounded by _____ Secret Service agents at
                                    NUMBER

any given time, so you should feel _____ going anywhere. You
                                        ADJECTIVE

get your own personal chef, who will make you _____ every
                                                  TYPE OF FOOD

day if you want, and prepares special _____ for important
                                        TYPE OF FOOD (PLURAL)

guests. Fresh flowers are provided daily by a/an _____, and a
                                                      OCCUPATION

personal valet makes sure you look _____ from head to
                                        ADJECTIVE

_____. A vacation home called Camp _____ is
   PART OF THE BODY   PERSON IN ROOM

your place to privately _____ when you need to get away from
                            VERB

the _____ in DC. And best of all, after you leave your job,
       PLURAL NOUN

you still get paid two hundred thousand _____ a year for the
                                            PLURAL NOUN

rest of your life!

MAD LIBS® is fun to play with friends, but you can also play it by yourself! To begin with, DO NOT look at the story on the page below. Fill in the blanks on this page with the words called for. Then, using the words you have selected, fill in the blank spaces in the story.

Now you've created your own hilarious MAD LIBS® game!

STATE OF THE UNION

NOUN _____

ADJECTIVE _____

NUMBER _____

OCCUPATION (PLURAL) _____

PLURAL NOUN _____

NOUN _____

PLURAL NOUN _____

PLURAL NOUN _____

ADVERB _____

VERB ENDING IN "ING" _____

PLURAL NOUN _____

VERB ENDING IN "ING" _____

PART OF THE BODY _____

NOUN _____

ADJECTIVE _____

EXCLAMATION _____

MAD LIBS

STATE OF THE UNION

My fellow Americans, as the new _____ begins, I am

NOUN

_____ to say how much we've accomplished. _____

ADJECTIVE   NUMBER

new jobs have been created. Our _____ are earning

OCCUPATION (PLURAL)

more _____ than ever before. We have finally reformed our

PLURAL NOUN

_____ care system. Millions of _____ now have

NOUN   PLURAL NOUN

access to _____ that they _____ need. Across the

PLURAL NOUN   ADVERB

globe, America is _____ to ensure our safety and to

VERB ENDING IN "ING"

ensure that _____ are protected. But we have to keep

PLURAL NOUN

_____ if we are going to continue to flourish. I am

VERB ENDING IN "ING"

certain we can, if we work hand in _____ to achieve our

PART OF THE BODY

goals. The state of our _____ has never been more

NOUN

_____ . I think we can all collectively shout, " _____ !"

ADJECTIVE   EXCLAMATION

MAD LIBS® is fun to play with friends, but you can also play it by yourself! To begin with, DO NOT look at the story on the page below. Fill in the blanks on this page with the words called for. Then, using the words you have selected, fill in the blank spaces in the story.

Now you've created your own hilarious MAD LIBS® game!

ALL THE PRESIDENT'S

_____
PLURAL NOUN

VERB _____

NOUN _____

PLURAL NOUN _____

VERB _____

FOREIGN COUNTRY _____

FOREIGN COUNTRY _____

PLURAL NOUN _____

ADJECTIVE _____

VERB _____

NUMBER _____

PLURAL NOUN _____

VERB ENDING IN "ING" _____

TYPE OF FOOD _____

PLURAL NOUN _____

NOUN _____

VERB _____

MAD LIBS
ALL THE PRESIDENT'S

_____
PLURAL NOUN

The **president** is constantly surrounded by advisors who _____
VERB

for him or her every day. For example . . .

The **chief of staff** coordinates every _____ between the
NOUN

president and other _____ .
PLURAL NOUN

The **secretary of state's** job is to _____ all around the world
VERB

to places like _____ and _____ .
FOREIGN COUNTRY   FOREIGN COUNTRY

The **attorney general** oversees enforcement of all our _____ .
PLURAL NOUN

He or she is the most _____ legal officer in the United States.
ADJECTIVE

The **secretary of defense** must _____ all _____
VERB   NUMBER

branches of the military.

The **secretary of education** makes certain we educate our _____
PLURAL NOUN

properly by _____ on behalf of our schools.
VERB ENDING IN "ING"

The **secretary of agriculture** oversees farming, and the safety of your

favorite foods, like _____ .
TYPE OF FOOD

And the **secretary of** _____ might be the most important,
PLURAL NOUN

making sure that every _____ can _____ !
NOUN   VERB

Join the millions of Mad Libs fans creating wacky and wonderful stories on our apps!

Download Mad Libs today!